My Lenten Reflections

A Catholic Retreat for Every Lenten Season

(For ages 6 to 96)

Susan Lee

My Lenten Reflections

A Catholic Retreat for Every Lenten Season

(For ages 6 to 96)

Susan Lee

ISBN-10: 1548592730
ISBN-13: 978-1548592738
ISNB 9781545253793

Dedication

This book is dedicated to Our Lord Jesus and His Bride the Church, and our Blessed Mother. Thank you for leading me. May all seek you. This book is also dedicated to my children Skylar, Summer, and Thomas. I see God in your loving kindness. May you always seek the Lord and His Holy Church. This book was written for you so that you may know Jesus and His Bride better. Thank you for your feedback so that you and others are encouraged to read it! I also dedicate this book to my husband Alan who has sought and found the Lord. You have inspired me to walk closer with the Him. Thanks to Laura M. for encouraging me to pursue publication, and for your holy example.

Finally, this book is for all of the Young Disciples of Our Lady of the Rosary whom I have taught, that you may continue to be on fire for our Lord and His Bride, the Holy Catholic Church.

- With love from Miss Susan

Introduction

Your Catholic faith is where you can always go for the truth, for the right thing to do. It is perfect because its founder, Jesus, is perfect. "…and the truth will make you free." – John 8:32

This book is designed for people just learning the Catholic faith, or for those well versed in their faith. It is also designed to be a quick, daily read (each reading takes a few minutes or less), and is designed to be re-read every Lenten season, for all ages.

To use this book, simply begin reading on the Sunday before Ash Wednesday. Just read the page for the corresponding day of Lent (sometimes 2 pages). Ponder on the reflection for that day. After 40 days of Lent, and pondering our Lord, your prayer time may just become the part of your day you yearn for most!

Love, Miss Susan

My Lenten Reflections

Love, Miss Susan

My Lenten Reflections

Sunday Before Ash Wednesday

Get ready for Lent! This is the one time of year we devote ourselves to prayer, and a promise to start a new life in Christ. We do this once a year, but we should continue the prayer life that we commit to during Lent.

Lent is a time to renew our devotion to Jesus. We promise to pray every day for 40 days and the 10 Sundays during Lent. And once we are 14 years old, we do not eat meat on Fridays, and at 18, we fast on Ash Wednesday and Good Friday.

Also, promise Jesus that you will either give something up or do something charitable for these 40 days. You can rest from this on the Sundays of Lent. So, if you give up candy, you can have it on the Sundays of Lent, but only have what you normally would; not a week's worth!! Do not substitute candy for cupcakes. Lovingly keep your promise to Jesus who loves you so much! If you forget, and eat candy, and it is not Sunday, go to Confession.

Love, Miss Susan

Monday Before Ash Wednesday

Why is Lent 40 days before Easter?
(46, if we include Sundays)

Because many times of preparation and purification that occur in the Bible are for 40 days, years, etc., namely because Jesus went alone in the desert and fasted for 40 days as soon as He was baptized, just before He began public ministry. So we think about Jesus and His own fasting, prayer, and preparation time for public ministry, and unite our time with His. Jesus spent these 40 days thinking about you, yes, YOU, during this time, how much He loved you and wanted you to be in Heaven with Him so badly that He willingly laid down His life, and prayed for the strength to go through His Passion, 3 years later in order to save you from your sins and get you into Heaven with Him.

God really knows what He is doing because when people do something for 40 days in a row, it becomes a habit! Isn't it interesting that Lent is 40 days?! (...because we have off on Sundays during Lent. Including Sundays, the Lenten season is a total of almost 50 days long.)

Love, Miss Susan

Tuesday Before Ash Wednesday

What is Mardi Gras?

Mardi Gras (some people call it "Fat Tuesday") is a big celebration started by Catholics long ago. During the celebration, we eat and drink together because we know we will be fasting the next day, Ash Wednesday, and beginning a new life in Jesus over the full Lenten season, as Lent is a time of sacrifice. Mardi Gras is always held on Tuesday, the day before Ash Wednesday.

Love, Miss Susan

My Lenten Reflections

Ash Wednesday

Today, we go to Mass and get ashes on our foreheads in the sign of the cross. The priest says, "From ashes you came, and to dust you shall return." This means God created the first person, Adam, from the ground, and when we die, we return to the ground.

The ashes come from the burnt palms from last year's Palm Sunday. Fast today if you are between 14 and 65 years old. That means you can have 1 meal, and 2 small meals that together do not make another meal.

Don't forget that today is the first day of your sacrifice: If you have promised to give up candy for Lent, you start that today! Remember, God commands us to rest on Sundays. So on Sundays of Lent, you are supposed to enjoy a piece of candy (if that's your sacrifice) to further appreciate what Jesus has given for you.

Love, Miss Susan

Thursday After Ash Wednesday

How to Pray

Part A:

As you read these reflections each day, take time to spend time with our Lord and to pray. It's hard to know what we should do when we pray. This is an easy way to remember what steps to take and what to do to pray: **Wow, Oops, Thanks, and Please**.

Wow – This is when we adore God, and praise him for all of His wonders, and all the glorious things He has done and sacrificed for us. If you need help, you can simply read a Psalm. These are prayers of praise to God, and are found in the Bible.

Oops – This is when you confess your sins to God. The word "sin" means "missing the mark." Sin does not always mean evil; it simply means that we missed the mark of perfection which Jesus wants from us. So confess anything you did (or thought) that you think would hurt Jesus.

Tomorrow, we will learn about **Thanks and Please**.

Love, Miss Susan

My Lenten Reflections

Friday After Ash Wednesday

How to Pray

Part B:

Yesterday we learned details of Wow and Oops. Today we'll learn about Thanks and Please.

Thanks – This is when you thank God for all His blessings; either on your life or on the world or family or friends. Thank Him for your eyesight, food, friends, family, house, flowers, birds, your safety and your family's, etc. The sky is the limit!

Please – This is when you ask God for things. Usually we start off prayer asking for things. But if we first adore (wow), apologize (oops), and are grateful to Him (thanks), then He will be so happy to answer your requests. You can ask God to continue blessing your family with health, or help to pass a test, or for a sick person to get better, or something bad in the world to change for the better. God always answers prayers, but sometimes He might say "no"; sometimes He might say "Yes"; and sometimes He might say, "Yes, but you have to wait a while."

Love, Miss Susan

Saturday After Ash Wednesday

Where did the Bible Come from?
The Catholic Church!

All the Bishops of the entire world got together 3 times to decide which books should be part of the Bible.

- Council of Rome in 382 A.D.: The Canon was approved by the Pope.
- Council of Hippo in 393 A.D.: The Canon of Scripture was ratified.
- Council of Carthage in **397 A.D.**: The Canon of Scripture was officially ratified on August 28, 397 AD.

All 3 times, they determined that the same 73 "inspired books" would make up the Bible (the canon): 27 New Testament books, and 46 Old Testament books. (In 1517, Martin Luther founded Protestantism and removed over 7 books, including 200 verses from Daniel and 100 from Esther, so Protestants use a smaller Bible.)

Love, Miss Susan

First Sunday of Lent

The Catholic Church is the Pillar and Foundation of Truth!

1 Timothy 3:15 states, *"if I am delayed, you may know how one ought to behave in the household of God, which is **the church** of the living God, **the pillar and bulwark of the truth**"*.

The Church can exist without the Bible, but the Bible cannot exist without the Church:
2 Thessalonians 2:15 states, *"So then, brothers and sisters, stand firm and hold fast to the **traditions** that you were **taught** by us, either **by word of mouth** or by our letter."*

And since we had no Bible for 397 years after Christ, Christians had only the Catholic Church!!! No Bible existed until 397 AD, but the Catholic Church did!

Love, Miss Susan

Monday, First Week of Lent

Jesus founded one church with Peter as the first Pope: Matthew 16:18-19

Matthew 16:18a He told Peter, *"...you are Peter, and on this rock I will build my <u>church</u>"*. He did not say "churches".

Also, Jesus spoke Aramaic, not Greek, & used "Kepha" to say both "Peter" & "rock": "You are Kepha and upon this kepha I will build my church."

We have had an unbroken line of Popes ever since this day.

Matthew 16:18b-19a *"and the gates of Hades will not prevail against it. I will give you the keys to the kingdom of heaven..."* Peter is given authority over heaven!!

Matthew 16:19b: *"...whatever you bind on earth will be bound in heaven, and whatever you loose on earth will be loosed in heaven."* Peter's given power over heaven that God must abide by! So we KNOW that the Holy Spirit guides the Pope – because God would never allow error in heaven.

Love, Miss Susan

Faith AND Works Needed For Salvation:
James 2:14-26

14 <u>What good is</u> it, my brothers..., if you say you have <u>faith but do not have works</u>? Can faith save you?...17 So <u>faith by itself, if it has no works, is dead</u>...19 ... <u>Even the demons believe</u> – and shudder. **(So the demons have faith. But they are not saved!)** *20 Do you want to be shown, <u>you senseless person, that faith apart from works is barren</u>? 21 Was not our ancestor <u>Abraham justified by works</u> when he offered his son Isaac on the altar?* **(Abraham is justified by <u>works</u>; not by faith!)** *22 You see that **<u>faith was active</u> along with his works, and** <u>faith was</u> **brought to completion by the works**. ...24 ...a person is <u>justified by works</u> and <u>not by faith alone</u>... 26 For just as **the body without the spirit is dead, so <u>faith without works is also dead</u>**.*

This declares that:
"body" is compared to **"faith"**, and
"spirit" is compared to **"works"**.

Love, Miss Susan

My Lenten Reflections

Losing Your Salvation

John 8:31b–32 - *"**If** you **continue** in my word, you are truly my disciples; and you will know the truth, and the truth will make you free."*

You can only say "**if** you continue in my word" to someone who is <u>already saved</u>! You can't "continue" something if you are not already there! Jesus tells saved people that they will be saved **if** they continue in His word.

Note that "if" is a powerful word. Jesus states that if, and only if, you continue in His word, you will know the truth; not "once saved always saved".

Don't forget to pray today: Wow, Oops, Thanks, & Please.

Love, Miss Susan

Thursday, First Week of Lent

Why Do We Call Priests "Father"?

Jesus said, in James 2:21 (NASB), *"Was not **Abraham our father** justified by works when he offered up his son Isaac on the altar?"* But Jesus also said, *"Do not call anyone on earth your father"* in <u>Matthew 23:9</u> (NASB). Was Jesus confused? No – when Jesus said, "Call no man father", He was speaking to the Pharisees about calling the hypocrite teachers "father" as an equal with God. "Our fathers" is stated at least 20 times in the New Testament. It refers to those who teach us about our Lord.

Don't forget to pray today: Wow, Oops, Thanks, & Please.

Love, Miss Susan

Friday, First Week of Lent

Why Do We Pray to Saints?

We Catholics are asking for Saints' Intercession (Praying to Saints). – Not worshipping them. Prayers from the Saints on our behalf are more powerful than our earthly friends/family who pray for us because the Bible states that the prayers of a righteous person carry more weight than prayers of others: James 5:16 – *"Therefore confess your sins to one another, and pray for one another, so that you may be healed. The prayer of the righteous is powerful and effective."* Yet Romans 3:10 states there are no righteous people. That means that <u>the only righteous people that James 5:16 can be talking about are those in heaven: angels, saints, and Mary</u>. And because of Jesus' promise of eternal life, the saints are not dead, but alive! So just as you ask your friends and family to pray for you, so can you ask the saints! They are part of your family too.

Love, Miss Susan

Saturday, First Week of Lent

How Do We Know That Mary is Sinless?

Genesis 3:15, the Lord tells Satan that He *"will put enmity between you and the woman, and between your offspring and hers; ..."* This means that the ONLY WAY that enmity (or "opposition") could be the barrier between Mary and the devil is for Mary to be sinless. (Eve collaborated with the serpent so this verse cannot pertain to Eve.)

Also, Luke 1:28 (RSVCE), Angel Gabriel salutes Mary (the only human to be saluted by an angel), stating, *"Hail, full of grace"* – Grace has no sin. Thirdly, everything in the New Testament is better than, and fulfills the Old Testament. It is not possible that the "new Eve", Mary, would be lesser than Eve (who brought sin into the world). So if Eve was born without original sin, then the Mother of Jesus Christ, the son of God, was born without original sin.

Love, Miss Susan

Sunday, Second Week of Lent

If God allows you to suffer much, it's a sign that He has great designs for you and that He certainly intends to make you a saint.

– St. Ignatius of Loyola.

Don't forget to pray today: Wow, Oops, Thanks, & Please.

Love, Miss Susan

Monday, Second Week of Lent

Forgiveness

Then Peter came and said to him, "Lord, if another member of the church sins against me, how often should I forgive? As many as seven times?" Jesus said to him, "Not seven times, but, I tell you, seventy-seven times. – Matthew 18:21-22

Jesus means to tell us that we should always forgive. He even acts as though it should be automatic from us: "*And forgive us our sins, for we ourselves forgive everyone indebted to us*" – Luke 11:4

Forgiveness does not mean you say it's okay for the person to hurt you. But it brings you closer to God and allows you to feel mercy for the person who hurt you.

The person who hurt you might feel so bad for what they did. Even if the person is not sorry, forgiveness releases you from the hurt the person caused you, and takes away the anger you feel inside. When you feel angry, you might not treat your friends and family very nicely. Forgiveness stops the power of that hurt over you. Forgive because God loves every one of us, and if He can forgive them, so can you!

Love, Miss Susan

My Lenten Reflections

Tuesday, Second Week of Lent

Mary's last recorded words in the Bible

Mary commands the people in John 2:5b: *"Do whatever he tells you."* This is one way we honor Mary: The mother of Jesus Christ tells us that we are to do whatever Jesus tells us to.

Don't forget to pray today: Wow, Oops, Thanks, & Please.

Love, Miss Susan

Wednesday, Second Week of Lent

Purgatory

Nothing unclean can enter Heaven per Revelation 21:27 (NABRE) *"but nothing unclean will enter it, nor any (one) who does abominable things or tells lies..."* Yet we are all sinners and unclean: Romans 3:23 *"since all have sinned and fall short of the glory of God."* Therefore, there must be another place to go, after death and before entering Heaven, to get cleansed: Purgatory.

Praying St. Gertrude's prayer releases 1,000 souls from Purgatory, and they pay back the favor by praying for you! The prayer is:

Eternal Father, I offer Thee the Most Precious Blood of Thy Divine Son, Jesus, in union with the masses said throughout the world today, for all the holy souls in purgatory, for sinners everywhere, for sinners in the universal church, those in my own home, and within my family. Amen.

Love, Miss Susan

Thursday, Second Week of Lent

Jesus wants a Guide over all the Church!

Part A:

Peter is mentioned about 170 times in the Bible. All other apostles combined are only mentioned about 95. This again shows that Peter had a higher importance than the other apostles.

- Throughout the Bible, all the other apostles look at Peter as the leader of their group. The apostles always look to him for direction, even after Jesus' resurrection.

- Luke 22:31-32 shows that all of the apostles would be attacked by Satan, but that Jesus prays for Peter especially so that Peter may show everyone the way: *"Simon, Simon, listen! Satan has demanded to sift **all of you** like wheat, but **I have prayed for you that your own faith** (meaning Peter alone) may not fail; and you, when once you (just Peter) have turned back (because Peter will stray away for a little while), **strengthen your brothers** (meaning the apostles)."*

Love, Miss Susan

Friday, Second Week of Lent

Jesus wants a Guide over all the Church!

Part B:

a. After His Resurrection, Jesus commands Peter to tend to his flock in His absence. John 21:17 (NABRE) *'He said to him the third time, "Simon, son of John, do you love me?" Peter was distressed that he had said to him **a third time**, "Do you love me?" and he said to him, "Lord, you know everything; you know that I love you." (Jesus) said to him, "Feed my sheep."'* Peter would never then, after receiving that command from Jesus, leave that flock without a shepherd. Therefore, successors of Peter (popes) were commanded by Jesus.

Don't forget to pray today: Wow, Oops, Thanks, & Please.

Love, Miss Susan

Saturday, Second Week of Lent

St. Ignatius of Antioch
and the Word "Catholic"

Ignatius of Antioch was born in 50 AD. He was ordained by Peter and taught by the disciple Paul and Apostle John. He was the second bishop of Antioch, after Peter. He is thought to be the child who Jesus took into His arms in Mark 6:35. He lived in time of great Christian persecution. He inspired hope and strength in his people. He hoped to receive full discipleship through being martyred (killed for his faith). Roman authorities arrested him and sent him to Rome to be executed. Ignatius recorded everything that happened on his way to be martyred in "Martyrium Ignatii".

Along his journey, people cheered for him. He wrote 7 very respected letters ("epistles") to Christians. In the Epistle to the Smyrnaeans 8, he wrote, "You must all follow the bishop as Jesus Christ follows the Father, ... Wherever the bishop appears, let the people be there; just as wherever Jesus Christ is, there is the **Catholic** Church". This was the 1st record of the word "Catholic". Remember, in 50 AD, there was only one group of Christians, not many different Christian religions, and this one group of Christians called themselves Catholic.

Ignatius was killed by the Romans with wild animals sometime between 98 AD and 117 AD. So it is apparent that the word "Catholic" was already in common use by Christians even before 98 AD. St. Ignatius is honored as a soldier, athlete, apostle, bishop, and martyr of Christ.

Love, Miss Susan

My Lenten Reflections

**The Catholic Church has one set of rules
that you can count on to guide you.**

We know we can trust this one set of rules because:

- The Catholic Church is over 2,000 years old and has never changed its doctrine.
- It compiled the Bible in 397 AD for the world.
- It existed for 397 years before the Bible!
- The Bible says the Church is *"the pillar and bulwark of truth."* – 1 Timothy 3:15
- The Church cannot be the pillar and foundation of truth if it teaches error.
- Ephesians 4:3-6 talks about one set of rules keeping Christians united: *"striving to preserve the unity of the spirit through the bond of peace: one body and one Spirit, as you were also called to the one hope of your call; one Lord, one faith, one baptism; one God and Father of all, who is over all and through all and in all."*

Love, Miss Susan

My Lenten Reflections

Monday, Third Week of Lent

The 4 Marks of the Church:

The Nicene Creed was made hundreds of years ago by our Catholic bishops to help you remember what we believe. The creed discusses the 4 Marks of the Church:

1. One,
2. Holy,
3. catholic (universal), and
4. Apostolic

Over the next 4 days, we will talk about each mark of the Church.

Don't forget to pray today: Wow, Oops, Thanks, & Please.

Love, Miss Susan

Tuesday, Third Week of Lent

The Church is One

God only wants one Christianity. Jesus prayed for unity. Hear what Ephesians 4:2-6 is saying to you: *"with all humility and gentleness, with patience, bearing with one another in love, 3 making every effort to* **maintain the unity of the Spirit** *in the bond of peace. 4 There is* **one body and one Spirit,** *just as you were called to the one hope of your calling, 5* **one Lord, one faith, one baptism, 6 one** *God and Father of all, who is above all and* **through all and in all.***"* Jesus created/founded one Church, the Catholic Church. The Church is one in the Holy Spirit, who is inside those who believe in Jesus, the Lord.

Love, Miss Susan

Wednesday, Third Week of Lent

The Church is Holy

The Church is holy because it is in union with Jesus who is the source of holiness. The Catholic Church leads others to holiness through the Holy Spirit. We can see the holiness of the members of our Catholic family, especially the Saints. They made many sacrifices for the world out of love and holiness. Look up St. Therese the Little Flower, or Saint Anthony, St. Bernadette, St. Bosco, St. Rita, St. Benedict. There are countless holy people in our faith.

Don't forget to pray today: Wow, Oops, Thanks, & Please.

Love, Miss Susan

My Lenten Reflections

The Church is Catholic

The word "catholic" means "universal", or "for everyone everywhere".   The Catholic church is universal in 2 ways:

- Because all who are baptized are part of the Church, and the Church provides salvation.   So, Catholics can go to heaven.
- Because the mission of the Church is to proclaim the good news of Jesus Christ to the entire world.

Don't forget to pray today: Wow, Oops, Thanks, & Please.

Love, Miss Susan

My Lenten Reflections

Friday, Third Week of Lent

The Church is Apostolic

The Church's tradition is 2,000 years old and is traced back directly to the apostles. The Pope and bishops are the successors (or descendants or replacements) of the apostles. The Holy Spirit preserves and continues the teaching of the apostles through the priests who can become bishops.

Don't forget to pray today:

Eternal Father, I offer Thee the Most Precious Blood of Thy Divine Son, Jesus, in union with the masses said throughout the world today, for all the holy souls in purgatory, for sinners everywhere, for sinners in the universal church, those in my own home, and within my family. Amen.

Love, Miss Susan

Saturday, Third Week of Lent

True Presence/The Eucharist

Exactly one year prior to the last supper, at Passover, Jesus said 6 times in John 6 that we must eat His flesh and drink His blood. It is the only thing said more than 3 times in a row in the Bible. If it was only symbolic, why didn't Jesus explain this so that the hundreds wouldn't leave? One year later, at the Passover of the last supper, Jesus states again in Luke 22:19 (NASBRE), knowing these are His last words with His 12, *"This **is** my body...**Do** this in memory of me."* It's a command. Also, 1 Corinthians 11:27 states, *"Whoever, therefore, eats the bread or drinks the cup of the Lord in an unworthy manner will be answerable for the body and blood of the Lord."* If it were only symbolic, no one could be *"answerable for the body and blood of the Lord"*. And it could not even be eaten/drunk in an unworthy manner unless it was Jesus!

Love, Miss Susan

Sunday, Fourth Week of Lent

Let nothing disturb you; Let nothing frighten you.   All things are passing. God never changes. Patience obtains all things. Nothing is wanting to him who possesses God. God alone suffices.

-   Bookmark found in St. Teresa of Avila's prayer book.

Monday, Fourth Week of Lent

Power to Apostles:
Confession & Forgiving/Retaining Sins

Parts A and B: *John 20:21-23*: (This is after Jesus' Resurrection, so He is giving commands for how his Church is to be run from here on out.)

Part A:

21 Jesus said to them again, "Peace be with you. _As the Father has sent me, so I send you_.

- This means He is giving the apostles the same exact authority he had been given by God. Jesus wanted his teachings to live on for eternity, which it does via the Catholic Church's priests, the successors of the apostles.

Love, Miss Susan

Tuesday, Fourth Week of Lent

Power to Apostles:
Confession & Forgiving/Retaining Sins

Part B:

22 When he had said this, <u>he breathed on them</u> and said to them, "Receive the holy Spirit."

- The only other time God breathed on someone was on Adam and Eve to breathe life into them.
- God here breathes new life of the Holy Spirit into Peter and the apostles, and the power for them to retain and forgive sins.

23 "If you forgive the sins of any, they are forgiven them; if you retain the sins of any, they are retained."

- See, Jesus wanted/expected people to confess their sins! How could the apostles forgive or retain sins if no one was confessing their sins to them?
- The apostles were the first priests given authority to forgive sins, per this Bible verse.

Love, Miss Susan

My Lenten Reflections

Wednesday, Fourth Week of Lent

The Power of Confession

Of the 7 sacraments, reconciliation is one of the most powerful weapons against Satan. It is so powerful because Satan created sin. Forgiveness of sins makes them no longer a power to Satan, but a gift to Jesus Christ.

It is always good to go to Confession within 10 days of Easter. Easter is only about 10 days away, so go to Confession soon!

Don't forget to pray today: Wow, Oops, Thanks, & Please.

Love, Miss Susan

Thursday, Fourth Week of Lent

"...and the gates of Hades will not prevail against it"
– Matthew 16:18b

Jesus promised Peter, when He made him the Rock and first Pope, that hell would never destroy His Church. Let's see if this is true:

- The Roman Empire sought to destroy Jesus – Indeed, they killed Him, and 10 out of the 12 apostles. But the Catholic Church, started by Jesus and the 12 mere common men, is still here, and the Roman Empire is not.
- The Nazis and Communists tried to destroy Jesus' Church too from 1914-1991, but, of the 3, only the Church still prevails.

God keeps His promises! God will always be here for you, as will His Church.

Love, Miss Susan

Friday, Fourth Week of Lent

"I do choose"

A leper came to him begging him, and kneeling he said to him, "If you choose, you can make me clean." **Moved with pity**, *Jesus stretched out his hand and touched him, and said to him,* **"I do choose**. *Be made clean!"* **Immediately** *the leprosy left him, and he was made clean.*
- Mark 1:40-42; Matthew 8:2-3; and Luke 5:12-13

Look how loving Jesus is in this passage. His love pours out to us. All we need to do is ask for His love and help, as this man did. As it says here, Jesus "immediately" helps. Jesus does choose us – Do you choose Him?

Spend time with the Lord today and pray.

Love, Miss Susan

My Lenten Reflections

Saturday, Fourth Week of Lent

St. Thomas the Apostle

St. Thomas did not believe it when the apostles told him that Jesus had risen. He said, *"Unless I see the mark of the nails in his hands and put my finger into the nailmarks and put my hand into his side, I will not believe."*- John 20:25 (NABRE). Jesus tells him in John 20:29, *"... "Have you believed because you have seen me? Blessed are those who have not seen and yet have come to believe."*

But don't we all have a little bit of Thomas in us? Once, a man asked Jesus to heal his son, but Jesus said, *"...if you can't believe, all things are possible to those who believe."* The man said with tears in his eyes, *"Lord, I do believe. Help my unbelief."* – Mark 9:24. And Jesus healed his son.

It is okay to have doubts. You only need to confess them and keep coming back to the Lord. The one who doubted the most, Thomas, also was one of the apostles who loved Him very much. It was Thomas who said to the disciples, *"Let us also go, that we may die with him."* (John 11:16b) Jesus knows that we have doubts, but that we still love Him. He loves us and died for us even though we are sinners. *("But God proves his love for us in that while we still were sinners Christ died for us."* – Romans 5:8)

Love, Miss Susan

My Lenten Reflections

Sunday, Fifth Week of Lent

People are often unreasonable, irrational, and self-centered. Forgive them anyway.

If you are kind, people may accuse you of selfish, ulterior motives. Be kind anyway.

If you are successful, you will win some unfaithful friends and some genuine enemies. Succeed anyway.

If you are honest and sincere people may deceive you. Be honest and sincere anyway.

What you spend years creating, others could destroy overnight. Create anyway.

If you find serenity and happiness, some may be jealous. Be happy anyway.

The good you do today, will often be forgotten. Do good anyway.

Give the best you have, and it will never be enough. Give your best anyway.

In the final analysis, it is between you and God. It was never between you and them anyway.

    –St. Teresa, Calcutta, India

Love, Miss Susan

Monday, Fifth Week of Lent

A Refresher on Lent

Lent means springtime and is a 40-day journey to a change of heart.   Lent is the season beginning <u>Ash Wednesday and ending on (and includes) the Mass of the Lord's Supper</u> or "The Last Supper" on Holy Thursday. It is a solemn time for penance, prayer, and fasting, reflecting on how we can be more loving toward God and toward others.

<u>Purple</u> represents Lent. (There are 10 Sundays within this 40-day journey, so the Lord's Supper is actually 50 days after Ash Wednesday, but fasting is not required on those Sundays.)

Don't forget to pray today: Wow, Oops, Thanks, & Please.

Love, Miss Susan

Tuesday, Fifth Week of Lent

The Triduum begins on Holy Thursday, includes Good Friday, and ends after the Holy Saturday Easter vigil. These are the 3 holiest days of the year, before Jesus' Resurrection on Easter Sunday, the next day.

- The liturgical color for the Holy Thursday is white for the joyful events that this season remembers.
- The liturgical color for Good Friday is red for Jesus' passion and death.
- The liturgical color for Holy Saturday is white for the joy of Jesus' Resurrection the next day.

Love, Miss Susan

Wednesday, Fifth Week of Lent

Thief Saved by Faith and Works

Part A:

The thief who died on the cross next to Jesus was saved by his faith and three works while hanging next to Jesus on the cross:

- <u>First</u>, the man rebuked a sinner: He told the criminal next to him to stop badgering Jesus, that they had their just rewards, but that Jesus had done nothing to deserve this.
- <u>Second</u>, the man admitted, took responsibility, and was sorry for his sin (acts of confession), per the rebuking above.
- <u>Third</u>, he publicly stated who Jesus was, and publicly asked him to remember him in His Kingdom, publicly declaring his faith.

Tomorrow we'll talk about Jesus saying, **"Today** you will be with me in paradise."

Love, Miss Susan

Thursday, Fifth Week of Lent

> "Truly I tell you, today you will be with me in paradise."
> -   Luke 23:43

Part B:

What did Jesus mean by "today" when he told the thief who repented, "Today you will be with me in paradise"?

In Paradise, "today" is forever.   Jesus tells Mary Magdalene in John 20:17, after resurrecting, *"Do not hold on to me, because I have not yet ascended to the Father..."*   If Jesus himself had not ascended to the Father even after 3 days, then the thief could not have gotten to Paradise before Jesus. If "today" was 3 days ago, and Jesus had not gotten there yet, then "today" must have a different time span in Paradise.

Love, Miss Susan

My Lenten Reflections

Friday, Fifth Week of Lent

"If we really understood the mass, we would die of joy."

-   St. Jean Vianney

Don't forget to pray today: Wow, Oops, Thanks, & Please.

Love, Miss Susan

Saturday, Fifth Week of Lent

<u>Jesus last words</u>: John 19:26-27
When Jesus saw his mother and the disciple whom he loved standing beside her, he said to his mother, "Woman, here is your son." Then he said to the disciple, "Here is your mother." And from that hour the disciple took her into his own home.

Jesus' last words are especially significant. He is commanding the world that Mary is our mother by disciple John's example. He gave Mary the same command that we are all her children.

Mary did not have any other sons because: Jewish people asked only blood brothers to take care of their parents. Since Jesus was Jewish, He would have honored His brother this way, if He had one.

There was no Jewish word for cousin, nephew, etc. "Brother" was used to for all kin. If Jesus had as many blood brothers in the Bible as "brother" is stated in relation to Jesus, then he would have had 90 blood brothers!

Love, Miss Susan

Palm Sunday

Palm Sunday is when Jesus came to Jerusalem and the people there celebrated by throwing palms.

There is great significance for Jesus entering upon a donkey. Remember when David proclaimed himself to be the new King thousands of years earlier, he entered the town on the last king's donkey! Now Jesus comes into Jerusalem in the same style as David, the King that the Jews' line comes down from. He is showing that He is the new King of the Jews.

This made the Pharisees very angry because they were the powerful Jews during Jesus' time, and they already feared Jesus because he challenged whether they really were godly men. Now Jesus arrives like King David did, showing that He is the new King! God Himself! This is why the people turned from loving Him so much on this day to killing Him five days later: The Pharisees created a big uprising against Jesus.

Love, Miss Susan

Monday of Holy Week

The Mass

Every aspect of the Mass, every word except the homily, incense, altar, etc. is directly from the Bible.

Examples:
1. **"The Lord be with you"** – 2 Thessalonians 3:1
2. **"Lord, have mercy (Kyrie)"** – Matthew 17:15
3. **"Lift up your hearts"** – Lamentations 3:41
4. **"Holy, holy, holy (Sanctus)"** – Revelation 4:8
5. **"Lord I am not worthy that you should enter under my roof..."** – Matthew 8:8
6. **Incense** from Revelation; etc.

Heaven and earth actually become one. It is being in the presence of Jesus, communing in the Eucharist, it is true worship, and it is 2,000 years old. The very first Christians conducted the mass in people's houses. The book of Acts shows how the first Christians (aka Catholics) celebrated mass, as it is done today.

After 3 years of attending Sunday masses, you have read through the entire Bible. For the last 2,000 years, we have read the same four Bible passages together (Old Testament reading, Psalm reading, New Testament reading, Gospel reading), and all around the world, the same 4 are being read that day.

Love, Miss Susan

Tuesday of Holy Week

Catholics are the light of the world!

Matthew 5:14-15
14 You are the light of the world. A city built on a hill cannot be hid. 15 No one after lighting a lamp puts it under the bushel basket, but on the lampstand, and it gives light to all in the house.

Only one Church stands out as the light of the world –
The only one that has:
- priests,
- confessions,
- the Eucharist,
- the Vatican,
- a pope,
- the mass, and
- 7 Sacraments.

Love, Miss Susan

Wednesday of Holy Week

Remember, the Triduum begins Tomorrow

The Triduum is the 3 days beginning at sundown on Holy Thursday, Good Friday, and Holy Saturday through evening prayer on Easter Sunday. These are the 3 most holy days of the year for all Christians.

Don't forget to pray today: Wow, Oops, Thanks, & Please.

Love, Miss Susan

Holy Thursday

Holy Thursday is the celebration of the Lord's Supper, and commitment of service to others, symbolized by Jesus & the apostles washing each other's feet. This is the night that Judas betrayed Jesus during the Passover meal, Jesus' last meal.

Holy Thursday is the day that Jesus instituted the Eucharist at the Last Supper. He knew that this was His very last day to be with the apostles before being crucified. If you knew it was the last day you would be with your family, would you say important words? You would, as Jesus did. He said, *"This is my body, which is given for you. Do this in remembrance of me."* (Luke 22:19)

At their Passover meal exactly 1 year earlier, Jesus told the multitudes 6 times to eat His flesh & drink His blood. No one understood, and all but the apostles left. Now, at the Last Supper, the apostles are beginning to understand that the Eucharist/Jesus would be the sacrifice (now a **pure sacrifice**) from now on. No more sacrificing lambs on Passover, but instead, the Eucharist. Without the Eucharist, Jesus' crucifixion would only have been an execution, not a sacrifice.

Love, Miss Susan

Good Friday

This is the day that the Lord was crucified, and then died on the cross at 3 p.m. There is no mass, but we venerate the cross, and proclaim Scripture and Holy Communion. No decorations are in Church, and we fast and do not eat meat. (See "Ash Wednesday" for details.)

It is called Good Friday because, even though Jesus dies this day, He fulfills all of God's promises in the Old Testament, and He makes a heaven for us.

An excellent Novena (i.e., 9-day prayer) to begin today is the Divine Mercy Chaplet. It only takes 5 minutes and is done at 3pm every day for 9 days from Good Friday, until the Sunday after Easter.

Remember, Lent is over today, but since it is a day of fasting, you can only have candy (if that's what you gave up) starting tomorrow!

Love, Miss Susan

Holy Saturday

Many Catholics go to the Easter Vigil. It begins in the evening and goes well into the night. New Catholics are baptized and confirmed into the Church on this day. It is a very joyous mass. The liturgical color is white.

Some Catholic trivia:

<u>The Catholic Church started the standards</u> for most of what we take for granted today. The Catholic Church started the **first universities, museums, hospitals, courtrooms, the studies of seismology, linguistics, botany, entomology, astronomy, agricultural science, etc.**

<u>Coined the phrases</u> "holy smoke", "holy mackerel", "X marks the spot", "integrity", "utopia", "litany", "devil's advocate", "propaganda", "epiphany", "apple of my eye", "knock on wood", "cross your fingers", etc.

<u>Roots of these are traced back to the Catholic Church</u>: golf, tennis, bowling, fishing, dumbbells, Olympics, chess, playing cards, steeplechase, piñatas, lacrosse, dominoes, Mother's Day, St. Valentine's Day, Groundhog Day, etc. (Reference: *"Why Do Catholics Eat Fish on Friday?"* by Michael P. Foley)

<u>J.R.R. Tolkein</u> was the author of "The Hobbit" and "Lord of the Rings". His novels have deep Catholic meanings. There are many college courses devoted to the Catholicism represented in his books.

Love, Miss Susan

My Lenten Reflections

Easter Sunday

He is risen!! He made a heaven for us and overcame the fall of Adam and Eve!

Jesus first appeared to three women before appearing to the apostles. Even so, He chose 12 men for His apostles. So we see that Jesus had a special role for both men and women. Therefore, only men can be priests, and only women can be nuns. Both have an equal and beautiful role whether they choose married life or religious life, as shown by Jesus' choices of who He appeared to and who He chose for apostles.

(Jesus stayed with the apostles **40 days**. Then He ascended into heaven. **Ten days** later, the Holy Spirit came as tongues of fire, and all Christians of different languages could understand each other! This is called Pentecost and is the birthday of the Catholic Church. So, the Easter season begins this evening and lasts **50 days**.)

Love, Miss Susan

My Lenten Reflections

Suggested Resources:
(For adults and children)

- **Catholic Answers** website
- **EWTN** TV, online, radio
- **Bible Christian Society** website by John Martignone
- **Crossroads Initiative** website by Marcellino D'Ambrosio
- **Lighthouse Catholic Media** (My favorite CDs: "Finding the Fullness of Faith" by Stephen Ray! "Detox" by Jason Evert.)
- **The Vatican or Holy See** website
- Crusades: CatholicEducation.org and IgnatiusInsight.com
- The Little Books of the Diocese of Saginaw
- Talks and books by Stephen Ray, Scott Hahn, Michael Barber, Edward Sri, John Martignone, Fr. Mitch Pacwa, Patrick Madrid, Fr. Michael Gaitley

Any resources approved by the Catholic Bishops have the following stamp: *"NIHIL OBSTAT: I have concluded that the materials presented in this work are free of doctrinal or moral errors"* and/or *"Imprimatur"*. So if you would like to do further study on the Catholic faith, any material that has this stamp is a perfect resource.

Translations of the bible approved by the United States National Council of Catholic Bishops (USNCCB) for private use by Catholics include:

- New Revised Standard Version, Catholic Edition, National Council of Churches (NRSVCE)
- New American Bible, Revised Edition (NABRE)
- Today's English Version, Second Edition, American Bible Society

Love, Miss Susan

My Lenten Reflections

About the Author

Susan Lee is a wife and mother of three. She has an MBA and has practiced Project Management, achieved the St. Elizabeth Ann Seton Award and Silver President's Volunteer Service Award. She is currently a full-time mother, and a catechist at Our Lady of the Rosary Catholic Church in Land O'Lakes, FL.

Love, Miss Susan

Made in United States
North Haven, CT
03 March 2023

33522569R00036